WHAT IF YOU H[...]

T. rex Teeth!?

And Other Dinosaur Parts

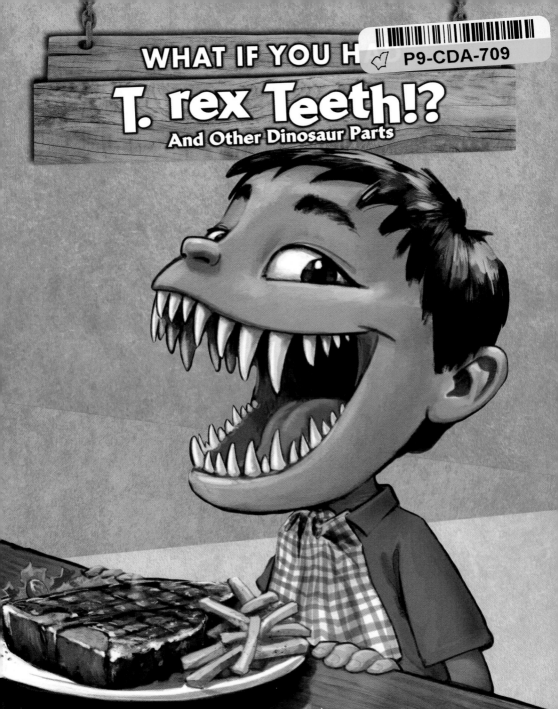

by **Sandra Markle**

Illustrated by

Howard McWilliam

Scholastic Inc.

For Betsy Lobmeyer
and the children
of Plymell
Elementary School
in Garden City,
Kansas.

A special thank-you to Skip Jeffery for his loving support during the creative process.

The author would like to thank the following people for sharing their enthusiasm and expertise: Dr. David Button, North Carolina State University and North Carolina Museum of Natural Sciences, Raleigh, North Carolina (*Brachiosaurus*); Dr. Kenneth Carpenter, Museum Director, USU Eastern Prehistoric Museum (*Ankylosaurus*); Dr. Greg Erickson, Florida State University, Tallahassee, Florida (*Tyrannosaurus rex*); Dr. Andrew Farke, Raymond M. Alf Museum of Paleontology, Claremont, California (*Stegosaurus* and *Triceratops*); Dr. Denver W. Fowler, Dickinson Museum Center, North Dakota (*Velociraptor*); Dr. Stephan Lautenschlager, University of Birmingham, Birmingham, United Kingdom (*Therizinosaurus*); Dr. Jordan Mallon, Canadian Museum of Nature, Ottawa, Ontario, Canada (*Edmontosaurus* and identification of dinosaur scientific names for timeline); Dr. Adam Marsh, Petrified Forest National Park, Holbrook, Arizona (*Dilophosaurus*); Dr. John Scannella, Dr. John R. Horner Curator of Paleontology, Museum of the Rockies, Bozeman, Montana (*Triceratops*); Dr. Paul Sereno, University of Chicago, Chicago, Illinois (*Spinosaurus*); Dr. Tom Williamson, New Mexico Museum of Natural History, Albuquerque, New Mexico (*Parasaurolophus*).

Photos ©: 4: Science Photo Library/Mark Garlick/Getty Images; 5 inset: Phil Degginger/age fotostock; 8: Leonello Calvetti/Getty Images; 9 inset: Justin Tallis/Getty Images; 10: CoreyFord/Getty Images Plus; 11 inset: Francois Gohier/ardea.com/age fotostock; 13 inset: Andy Crawford/Dorling Kindersley/Getty Images; 15 inset: Evgeniy Mahnyov/Alamy Stock Photo; 16: José Antonio Peñas/Science Source; 17 inset: Millard H. Sharp/Science Source; 19 inset: Ken Lucas/Getty Images; 20: Stocktrek Images/Getty Images; 21 inset: Oleksiy Maksymenko/age fotostock; 23 inset: Mohamad Haghani/Alamy Stock Photo; 24: XiaImages/Getty Images; 25 inset: dpa picture alliance/Alamy Stock Photo; 31 left: Ben Molyneux/Alamy Stock Photo. All other photos © Shutterstock.com.

Text copyright © 2023 by Sandra Markle
Illustrations copyright © 2019 by Howard McWilliam

Library of Congress Cataloging-in-Publication Data available

ISBN 978-1-338-84731-4

10 9 8 7 6 5 4 3 2 1   23 24 25 26 27

Printed in the U.S.A. 40
This edition first printing: February 2023

What if one day, you felt a bit STRANGE?
One part of your body was VERY different.
What if there was a DINOSAUR part in its place?

TYRANNOSAURUS REX

Tyrannosaurus rex
had a big TOOTHY bite.
Each of its seven-inch-long teeth
had sharp, jagged edges.
Picture a mouthful of giant
steak knives!

With *Tyrannosaurus rex* teeth, you'd cut up your whole meal in one bite!

FACT

Sharp teeth show it was a meat eater. It ate other animals.

VELOCIRAPTOR

(veh-LOSS-ih-RAP-tor)

Velociraptor had a swordlike claw on each hind foot. Perfect for grabbing its dinner!

With *Velociraptor* toes, you would open presents in a flash.

FACT

It had sharp meat-eater teeth, too.

STEGOSAURUS

(STEG-uh-SAWR-us)

Stegosaurus was a plant eater
with a built-in weapon.
Its tail tip had two-foot-long spikes.
So, enemies got spiked-tail SMACKS!

With *Stegosaurus* tail spikes, you could toast marshmallows for everyone.

FACT

Its tail was made up of lots of tailbones.
That let it easily swing and strike.

PARASAUROLOPHUS

(par-ah-SAWR-OL-uh-fus)

Parasaurolophus had a head crest that was up to five feet long. X-rays show the crest was full of breathing tubes from throat to tip. What WILD noises did it blast out?

With a *Parasaurolophus* head crest, you would lead the school marching band.

FACT

Different crest lengths gave each *Parasaurolophus* its own voice.

ANKYLOSAURUS

(ang-KILE-uh-SAWR-us)

Ankylosaurus was built like a tank.
Bone plates gave it body armor.
A helmetlike skull kept its head safe.
Some even had armored eyelids!

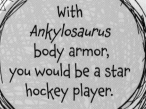

With *Ankylosaurus* body armor, you would be a star hockey player.

FACT

A club-tipped tail kept enemies away.

BRACHIOSAURUS

(BRACK-ee-uh-SAWR-us)

Brachiosaurus had a neck close to 30 feet long.
It was the perfect treetop plant eater.
But it had a SUPERLONG swallow!

With a *Brachiosaurus* neck, you could easily see a movie from any seat.

FACT

Its neck bones were full of holes. That made its neck light enough to lift.

15

THERIZINOSAURUS

(thair-uh-ZEEN-uh-SAWR-us)

Therizinosaurus had two-foot-long front claws.
Just what this plant eater needed to tug leafy branches close enough to eat.

With *Therizinosaurus* claws, you would turn hedges into art.

FACT

It had tiny plant-eater teeth.

EDMONTOSAURUS

(ed-MON-tuh-SAWR-us)

Edmontosaurus was a plant-eating machine!
It had shovel-shaped jaws for scooping.
A hard beak was just right for snipping.
And 700 teeth made chewing easy.

With *Edmontosaurus* shovel jaws, you would win every food-eating contest.

FACT

Fossils show it had six-sided scales.

TRICERATOPS

Triceratops must have
put up a good fight.
This plant eater had a big nose horn.
Each brow had an even longer horn.
Its head also had a helmetlike shield.
So, it was both armed and armored!

20

With *Triceratops* horns, you would carry groceries in just one trip.

FACT

Triceratops's helmet even had a neck guard.

DILOPHOSAURUS

(dye-LO-fuh-SAWR-us)

Dilophosaurus had long hind legs and three-toed feet. Just eight feet tall, it would have been light and fast. It likely made quick turns and BIG leaps to catch breakfast, lunch, and dinner.

With *Dilophosaurus* hind legs, you'd be a star dancer.

FACT

Dilophosaurus had meat-slicing teeth.

SPINOSAURUS

(SPY-nuh-SAWR-us)

Spinosaurus had a GIANT sail on its back.
Six-foot-long spines kept it upright.
No one knows for sure why it had its sail.
Maybe just to be a BIG show-off.

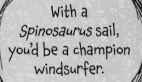

With a *Spinosaurus* sail, you'd be a champion windsurfer.

FACT

Its back feet toenails were GIANT, too.

What if you could keep a dinosaur part?

Which dinosaur part would be right for you?

Luckily, you don't have to choose.
This isn't the Age of Dinosaurs.

You're living NOW!
All your parts are people parts.
They are just what you need to be YOU!

WHY ARE THERE NO DINOSAURS TODAY?

No one knows for sure what happened.
Maybe a giant space rock struck Earth.
It kicked up dirt, making it dusty dark.
That killed plants, so plant eaters died.
Then meat-eater dinosaurs died.

TIMELINE

Not all dinosaurs lived at the same time.

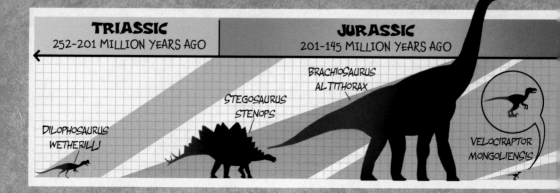

TRIASSIC	JURASSIC
252–201 MILLION YEARS AGO	201–145 MILLION YEARS AGO

DILOPHOSAURUS WETHERILLI

STEGOSAURUS STENOPS

BRACHIOSAURUS ALTITHORAX

VELOCIRAPTOR MONGOLIENSIS

Maybe volcanoes gave off deadly gas.
That would have killed dinosaurs, too.

Scientists think that whatever happened,
the Age of Dinosaurs ended around
66 million years ago.

**Here are two
dinosaur skeletons!**

Therizinosaurus

T. rex

CRETACEOUS
145–66 MILLION YEARS AGO

THERIZINOSAURUS
CHELONIFORMIS

PARASAUROLOPHUS
WALKERI

SPINOSAURUS
AEGYPTIACUS

EDMONTOSAURUS
ANNECTENS

ANKYLOSAURUS
MAGNIVENTRIS

TYRANNOSAURUS
REX

TRICERATOPS
PRORSUS

OTHER BOOKS IN THE SERIES